MW01172873

G. Zacarías

NM

CHEERS! WINES FROM NEW MEXICO

CHEERS! WINES
FROM NEW MEXICO

By: Guadalupe Zacarías

Facebook: Zacarias G Winesnm

Instagram: gwinesnm

E-mail: nmwines24@myyahoo.com

Registry: TXu 2-423-980

Acknowledgments

I want to express my gratitude to you, dear reader, for holding this book in your hands and giving me the opportunity to journey with you through the wonderful wine culture in the State of New Mexico.

My infinite thanks to the researchers, winemakers, and sommeliers who are part of this sensory journey, where each sip is a poem and each aroma a memory. To the farmers who care for the vines with love, and especially to the families who, generation after generation, help weave stories in every wine cellar.

Thank you to my three driving forces, Dorian, Ángel, and Carlos; you are my strength to move forward. To my mother, tireless and resilient, I thank her for being my example of perseverance. To my father, now a star in the firmament, I know he continues to guide me from the eternal. To my siblings who watch and support my steps, to my dear sisters Tere and Mitzia, my partners in laughter and tears, I thank you for never letting go of my hand on this journey called life.

I want to acknowledge the invaluable support of my editor, Víctor Juárez, who, with his patience and professionalism helped me improve the structure of this book.

Contents

Author's Foreword

Hello! I'm Guadalupe Zacarias, the author of the book "CHEERS! Wines from New Mexico." I consider myself a woman who finds pleasure in every new adventure I embark on, and I learn new and wonderful things from each of the places I visit.

On this occasion, it is my pleasure to share with you, throughout the following pages, the delightful experience I had when I visited New Mexico, and why I fell in love with its natural beauty and the warm welcome I received from its people from the moment I set foot in this wonderful land. With their constant kind words, warm gestures, and welcoming actions, it's easy to feel at home, a part of the community, which is why I chose to live here.

To this day, I am still impressed by the magnificent view of its landscapes, its vast expanses of land, its majestic mountains, and the skies, those stunning skies, blue during the day, yellow with orange and red hues in the evening. Everything is an invitation to explore and enjoy the pleasant sensation of freedom and clarity I feel while walking outdoors: it's as if nature is untouched by human influence, and the air I breathe is much fresher. This sense of peace and tranquility I have not found elsewhere.

And of course, I cannot talk about New Mexico without mentioning its excellent wines, which is what brings us together on this occasion, and deserves all my attention.

With this book, I seek to pay tribute to the passion and effort that local winemakers put into each bottle: from carefully cultivated vineyards to artisanal wineries, the region offers a unique and exquisite experience for wine lovers.

In summary, New Mexico is a hidden gem that deserves to be discovered, and I hope that my book inspires you to visit this beautiful region so that you fall in love with it just like I did.

Welcome

Monday, my day ended with extreme fatigue, both physically and mentally. My weekend was filled with strong positive and negative emotions, so I wanted to clear my mind and chose a place at random.

When I arrived and saw all the chairs occupied, I thought to myself: "I don't think this is the right place." It was one of those days when you feel like everything is against you and the world seems gray.

I sat outside for a few minutes, but something inside me called out. I entered again, this time through the other door, and as if it were an exclusive sign for me, I saw a single chair, right in front of the small stage, from where I could see whoever was singing at that moment.

I ordered the menu, checked the wines, and chose a red, but with a new flavor and combination that I didn't know. I was willing to enjoy one or two more songs, at most.

I drummed my fingers on the table while waiting for my glass. The music kept playing, but I didn't pay too much attention to it; I heard it in the background, like an echo among my overwhelming thoughts. The waitress brought me my wine... And it wasn't until I took the first sip that something strange happened: I felt that rich sweetness of the grape and the acidic taste of the wine dancing on my palate. At that moment, I could hear the sound of the guitar with major and minor chords clearly, and I could make sense of the magnificent and tuned voice of the musician, who was playing "Tennessee Whiskey".

Suddenly, the murmurs of the people ceased, everyone disappeared, it was as if only that place existed in the universe, that chair, that table, and me, savoring a delicious red wine. The music enveloped me with those seductive whispers as I continued with each sip. I breathed, I made an effort to clear my mind, to push away worries and intrusive thoughts. Time passed slowly, that interval tasted to me like I imagined the taste of glory.

Someone else got up to sing, accompanied by another guitarist.

I found myself back at the bar, the feeling of being unique disappeared, and although I heard the whispers and hums of others, that magical satisfying feeling remained in me that there was no better place to be than there. That was the excuse to order another glass.

The person behind the bar served drinks and refilled glasses, while chatting amiably with the customers. Unconsciously, I found myself answering questions and engaging in conversation, both with him and with other customers; it was the first time they had seen me in that place. And so, 3 hours passed, chatting, drinking, and having fun. When there was a minute left for the last song, I left the place, promising myself to return to that space that saved me from the chaos in my head.

I breathed in the fresh air and said to myself: "This is me; I am finally recovering myself after a long time." Just in

Photographer: Aaron Walterscheid

the ninth month, when it is time to harvest the crops of a year and prepare the land to sow again, the smile that once distinguished me, and that I had forgotten, finally returned to me. I filled myself with nighttime oxygen, fresh and clean. I was thankful to be in such a beautiful place, I felt blessed for everything I am, what I had lived, and what I had let go. I was excited, and in that state of frenzy from my rediscovery, I walked alone to my car, and drove back home. That day I slept like a baby, I felt calm again.

It's not the wine, it's not going out, it's not escaping reality, it's simply sitting there, aware of my emotions and accepting my present, reflecting on what is within my control, and what I can solve, and letting go of what does not depend on me, or overwhelms me. It's allowing myself to enjoy the music and travel with those passages, to be enveloped by those verses, by those caresses to the ear.

I want to tell the artists that, seeing them on stage, exposing their passion, executing with precision everything they have practiced for that moment, I am deeply grateful for their existence and for helping many lost souls, like me, to enjoy a good moment.

And here I am, coming to this place, virtually every Monday, with my phone on silent so as not to be interrupted, and savoring one or two glasses of a new wine.

Introduction

Thank you for taking the time to read this book, where I share my passion for the wines of New Mexico!

If you're looking for a unique experience in the world of wine, you've come to the right place.

Let me introduce you to the wines, their incredible history, and the winemaking process in this region steeped in winemaking tradition, which has been cultivated by generations of local and foreign producers who, like me, fell in love with this beautiful place and decided to stay to craft and preserve their wine offerings.

If you've ever tasted one of the wines from this region of the United States, you'll know that they are something special. Each sip is a delicious explosion of complex and sophisticated flavors that make their price worth it, and if you haven't had the pleasure of trying them yet, get ready for a sensory journey of discovery and delight.

Wine producers in New Mexico have perfected the art of viticulture, combining traditional techniques with modern methods to create wines that are, without exaggeration, true masterpieces. Their creations are the result of years of dedication and care: from grape selection, through the aging and bottling process, to distribution.

But it's not just the taste that makes New Mexico wines so special; it's also their history and the culture behind them. The vineyards are as rooted in the land as they are in the people who cultivate them, and it's reflected in every sip, turning each bottle into a work of art, an expression of the passion and love for wine that exists in this region.

In this book, I invite you to join me on a journey of discovery. We will explore the rich winemaking history and get to know the wines produced in New Mexico.

So, grab a glass, sit back, and enjoy the following pages: it will undoubtedly be inspiring and delicious. Cheers!

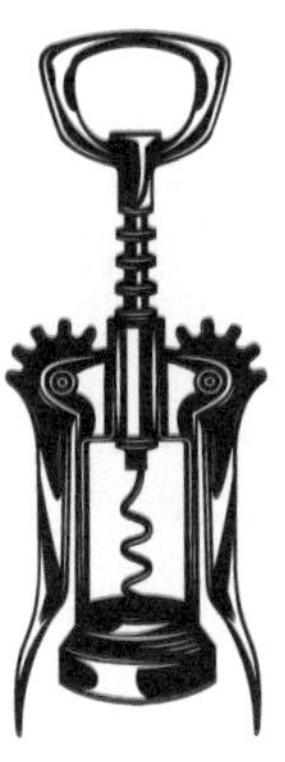

Photo: Río Grande Winery

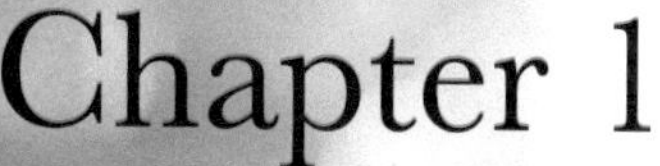

Chapter 1

Grapes in the Desert

"Wine is the only artwork you can drink.".

Luis Fernando Olaverri

Grapes in the Desert

Have you ever imagined vast expanses of land with an enormous quantity of juicy fruits and vibrant green leaves amidst the arid and dry desert? This place exists in the beautiful State of New Mexico, located in the Southwest of the United States, proudly called "the Land of Enchantment." Let me tell you a little about how the miracle of life emerged in these lands.

The history of New Mexico, according to records, dates back to the arrival of indigenous peoples over 10,000 years ago.

In the 16th century, Spanish explorers ventured into the region and established colonies in the area.

In 1821, New Mexico became part of Mexico after the country gained independence from Spain.

In 1846, during the Mexican American War, American troops occupied New Mexico, and the region became territory of the United States, joining as the 47th state. The indigenous and mestizo population of New Mexico fought for their independence and to preserve their culture and traditions in the 19th and 20th centuries.

American viticulture was born around 1629, with the first grape plantation brought by Franciscan monks from Spain, who sought to produce wines for religious ceremonies. The perfect place for their plantation was along the Rio Grande River; the birthplace of what is now a vast expanse of grape cultivation.

In 1872, a winery was founded by Jesuit priests, who settled in New Mexico and brought Italian techniques for wine production.

In recent decades, New Mexico has been recognized for its cultural diversity, gastronomy, natural landscapes, and rich history. Similarly, the number of vineyards and wineries has grown, as well as the variety of grape combinations. That's why you can find notes of traditions from France, Italy, and Germany in the state. This variety is present in the more than 50 wineries throughout the state.

The fusion of flavors in wine creation combines the rich wine history of the Old World with unique local influences from the region, resulting in distinctive and delicious wines that capture the essence of their place of origin.

Today, the wine industry in New Mexico is primarily concentrated in three areas: the Mesilla Valley, the Middle Rio Grande Valley, and Northern New Mexico. These areas have a semi-arid climate and soil suitable for viticulture.

Currently, this industry produces more than two million gallons annually, and the growth is continuous, thanks to the effort and dedication of all the people who come together in planting, caring for, and harvesting the grapes, as well as in wine production.

Photo: Personal library

Chapter 2

Grape Varieties in the Region

"A good wine is like a good film: it lasts a moment and leaves a taste of glory in your mouth; it is new with every sip and, as with films, it is born and reborn in each taster"

Federico Fellini

Grape Varieties in the Region

The grape varieties cultivated in New Mexico include Cabernet Sauvignon, Merlot, Chardonnay, Sauvignon Blanc, Riesling, Gewürztraminer, Albariño, Malvasía, Viognier, Vermentino, Muscat Blanc, Dolcetto, Malbec, Barbera, Montepulciano, and Tempranillo.

For those not involved in grape cultivation, they may all appear similar at first glance, but each one possesses unique characteristics and is destined for different wine production:

Red Grapes

Foto: Rio Grande Winery

• Dolcetto

Presents a moderate acidity and emits a suggestive perfume of flowers, along with an appealing sweet bitterness at the end, reminiscent of almonds.

• Montepulciano

Intensely red, it displays notes of red fruits and spices after aging in steel barrels.

• Malbec

Recognized for its deep violet-red color, it produces robust wines with high acidity, juiciness, and flavors of fruits such as plum, blackberry, and black cherry.

• Barbera

A grape variety with high yields, great resistance to diseases, which adapts very well to different climates and terrains where it can be found. Its wines have color, acidity, and sugars.

• Cabernet Sauvignon

Produces red wines that often have notes of dark fruits such as blackcurrant and plum, as well as hints of tobacco, green pepper, and spices.

• Merlot

Offers smoother wines, with flavors of ripe red fruits like cherry and raspberry, with hints of chocolate and spices.

• Tempranillo

Characterized by its early ripening, hence its name. It can produce a wide range of wines, from young and fruity wines to more structured red wines aged in oak.

White Grapes

Photo: Río Grande Winery

• Gewürztraminer

Produces highly aromatic and exotic white wines, with intense floral notes such as roses and lychees, along with spices such as ginger and pepper.

• Chardonnay

A versatile grape that can produce white wines in a wide range of styles, from fresh and fruity to rich and creamy.

Chardonnay wines have flavors of apple, pear, and citrus, with possible hints of vanilla and oak. It is also used in the production of sparkling wines.

• Sauvignon Blanc

Produces refreshing and aromatic white wines with herbal, citrus, and tropical fruit notes, which can have hints of freshly cut grass and gooseberry.

• Riesling

This highly aromatic grape produces white wines that can range from dry to sweet, with flavors of citrus and tropical fruits, as well as floral and mineral nuances. Additionally, it maintains a balance between acidity and sweetness.

• Malvasía

The white Malvasia grape is small and delicate, with intense flavor and aroma, traits that are reflected in the wines that come from it.

• Albariño

A moderately vigorous, robust, and fertile variety. It is characterized by early ripening and having small clusters of medium-sized grapes with thick skin. This variety adapts better to dry soils.

• Vermentino

Known for producing fresh, aromatic white wines with balanced acidity.

• Muscat Blanc

This grape is widely appreciated for its aromatic intensity, sweet flavor, and versatility, which allows it to be used in the production of various types of wines.

• Viognier

A white grape variety known for its aromatic characteristics and its ability to produce elegant and fragrant white wines.

Photo: Personal stock

Chapter 3

Process

"A great wine requires a madman to grow it, a wise man to watch over it, a lucid poet to craft it, and a lover who understands it."

Salvador Dalí

Process

This significant process can be compared to a "blank canvas" in the sense that each stage offers an opportunity for creativity and artistic expression, resembling the way an artist envisions the pristine surface of a piece of paper or a blank canvas, both ready to create a work of art. And, just as a painter can choose from a range of colors on their palette, similarly, a winemaker can select from the variety of grapes in the region to create their own masterpiece, and convey through this combination of flavors an emotion, a message, a touch of their place of origin.

As we can appreciate, this process is a combination of art and science, involving several key stages. To this, we must add the passion and commitment of those dedicated to this process, not forgetting the years of experience they have accumulated in the vineyards. This is how the perfect combination is achieved for the creation and selection of exquisite wines that we can enjoy with every sip.

Grape Selection and Planting

The grape selection and planting process for winemaking in New Mexico follows a careful and strategic approach, considering factors such as soil and climate, as the region experiences drastic changes throughout the seasons of the year.

Study of Climate and Soil

Before initiating grape planting, viticulturists in New Mexico, along with their respective winery staff, conduct a detailed analysis of the region's climate and soil. This includes evaluating factors such as temperature, precipitation, altitude, and sun exposure. Additionally, the information obtained helps determine which grape varieties will thrive best in that specific environment.

Variety Selection

Based on the information about climate and soil, grape varieties that are most likely to thrive in the region are chosen.

In New Mexico, it is common to find varieties resistant to heat and climatic variations, such as American and hybrid grapes.

Plant Propagation

Once the suitable varieties are selected, grape plants are obtained through the propagation of cuttings or grafts from mother plants, which have been shown to be productive and resilient in similar conditions.

Land Preparation

Before planting, the land is properly prepared by removing weeds and rocks, as well as improving soil drainage if necessary.

Seedtime

Grape plants are planted in rows, following a specific pattern. Holes are dug in the ground where the previously selected plants are placed, ensuring that the roots are well covered and protected.

Care and Maintenance

After planting, constant care is provided to the plants to ensure their healthy growth, including proper irrigation, fertilization, and pruning, as well as implementing management techniques to control pests and diseases that may affect the vineyards.

Vineyard Health

The vineyards of New Mexico, like in other wine-producing regions, can be affected by various pests and plant diseases,

which can have a negative impact on the health of the vines and the quality of the grapes. That's why a vast knowledge and experience in vineyard care and attention are needed.

The most common pest in vines is the Cicadellidae, also known as grape leafhopper. They measure less than 1/8 inch (1.4 cm) long and are capable of jumping from leaf to leaf to feed on the plant's sap, extracting nutrients and damaging the plant in the process.

The grape leaf skeletonizer refers to an insect that feeds on the tissue of grapevine leaves, leaving them with a skeleton-like appearance. Although it can cause aesthetic damage, it rarely poses a significant threat to the health of the plant or the quality of the grapes.

The so-called nematodes are microscopic roundworms that affect grape plants, and they can cause significant damage to the roots, which in turn can negatively affect the vine's growth, health, and production.

In smaller proportions, some insects such as grasshoppers, June beetles, flea beetles, snails, and mites, may infest grape plants.

To obtain healthy grapes, attention to detail in growth is essential, as grapes can be affected by various diseases:

Iron deficiency in plants can have several negative effects on vine growth and development, as well as on the quality of the grapes produced. Iron is an essential micronutrient for plants and plays a crucial role in various metabolic processes, including photosynthesis and chlorophyll production, which is important for the formation of plant

sugars. If its deficiency is not addressed, it can reduce yield, decrease fruit sugar content, and ultimately kill the vine.

Small leaves can become a problem, as well as root knot or rot. This is why those involved in grapevine care must be very attentive to changes in leaf color, as weak vines or a yellowish or reddish color may indicate a disease that needs to be addressed promptly.

It is important to highlight that pest management in the vineyards of New Mexico is based on a comprehensive approach, which combines cultural and biological practices, thus avoiding chemical control measures.

The most important aspect is the attention that viticulturists pay to vineyard conditions to take timely measures that prevent and control pests effectively, while minimizing environmental impacts.

Photo: Canva

Plant Training

As the plants grow, careful training is carried out to direct the growth of the vines: unwanted shoots are inspected and pruned, and the orientation of the branches toward a trellis or support system is signaled.

Harvest

Photo: Río Grande Winery

The harvest time in the state of New Mexico is a reason to celebrate; hundreds of people come together for this process, which is the foundation for winemaking. In places where the climate is warmer, the harvest for early varieties can begin in early August (summer), and as the season progresses, various types of grapes that ripen more slowly are harvested. Red and white grape varieties may have slightly different harvest times, and this is due to their ripening characteristics.

This process is a critical moment in wine production, as the grapes must be harvested at the optimum ripeness to ensure the quality and flavor of the wine.

Below you will find a description of the process.

Monitoring Grape Ripeness

Before harvest, grapes in the vineyard are constantly monitored. This includes analyzing the concentration of sugars, acids, and other components in the grapes to determine their ripeness. The taste and texture of the grapes are also evaluated to ensure they are at their best.

Plot Selection

Depending on the grape variety and vineyard conditions, specific plots may be selected for harvesting. Some areas may ripen faster than others, so it's important, for maximum quality, to harvest grapes at different times.

Harvesting Equipment

The necessary equipment for harvest is prepared, which may include pruning shears, electric shears, and mechanical equipment for larger vineyards. The equipment must be clean and in good condition to avoid damage to the grapes during harvest.

Manual Harvesting

In high-quality vineyards, manual harvesting is common; trained workers carefully pick the grapes by hand, selecting

only ripe grapes and leaving behind any that appear green or damaged.

Mechanical Harvesting

In larger vineyards, specialized machinery may be used for harvesting. The machines shake the vines, causing the grapes to fall, although this method may be less selective and should be used with caution to avoid damaging the grapes.

Transportation

Once harvested, the grapes are immediately transported to the winery. The time between harvest and transportation should be as short as possible to prevent oxidation and degradation of the grapes, which typically occurs very quickly.

Winery Processing

Upon arrival at the winery, the grapes undergo destemming, where the stems are removed to leave the grapes free and clean. Subsequently, they undergo crushing to extract the must (grape juice), which will be used for fermentation and wine production.

Final Destination of Grapes

Depending on the type of wine being produced, the grape juice may be directed to different processes. For white wines,

the juice is separated from the skins and fermented. For red wines, the grapes may undergo a maceration process before fermentation.

Grape harvest is an exciting and fundamental moment in wine production, and its success depends on careful attention to grape ripeness and quality. Grape selection is crucial as it will determine the quality and characteristics of the final wine.

Maceration

Maceration and fermentation are pivotal processes in winemaking, playing a fundamental role in extracting flavors, aromas, colors, and the structure of grapes. This process occurs post-harvest and is essential for achieving the diversity and complexity of the wines we know.

Depending on the type of wine desired, the juice and grape skins can be macerated together for a specific period. Throughout this stage, the natural yeasts present in the grapes, or added yeasts, convert the sugars in the juice into alcohol and carbon dioxide, a process known as "Alcoholic Fermentation."

Maceration involves allowing the grapes, sometimes with their seeds, to be in contact with the must (grape juice) for a set period before fermentation. This process is significant in producing red wines.

Importance of Maceration

During maceration, the pigments in the grape skins dissolve into the grape juice, imparting color to the wine. The duration of maceration can influence the intensity and hue of the resulting red wine.

Tannins, compounds primarily derived from grape skins and seeds, are extracted in this process and contribute to the structure and aging potential of the wine.

Additionally, maceration allows grape skins to release aromatic and flavor compounds into the juice, enhancing the diversity of aromas and flavors in the final wine.

Fermentation

Photo Canva

Fermentation is the process in which the sugars present in grape juice, under the action of yeast, are converted into alcohol and carbon dioxide. During fermentation:

I. Fermentation - Alcohol Production

Alcoholic fermentation is the process that converts the natural sugars in grapes into ethyl alcohol, which is the component that defines wine.

Fermentation generates heat, which can influence the flavor profile and aroma development of the wine. It's important to control the temperature during fermentation to avoid undesirable flavors, as this stage requires attention and knowledge. If not properly managed, a series of problems can arise, affecting both the aromas and flavors, as well as the texture and stability of the wine. Here are some:

I.I. Alcohol Production - Undesirable Flavors and Aromas:

High Temperatures

Excessively high temperatures can lead to the overproduction of volatile compounds, such as esters and alcohols, which can generate undesirable flavors and aromas in the wine, ranging from intense fruity notes to medicinal or solvent-like aromas.

Loss of Delicate Aromas

If the temperature is too high, the more delicate and subtle aromas in the wine may evaporate faster than they can develop, resulting in a wine with a less complex aromatic profile.

Violent Fermentation

High temperatures can also accelerate the fermentation rate, leading to potential aggressive or violent fermentation. This can result in spills and loss of grape juice.

On the other hand, excessively low temperatures can slow down or halt yeast activity, resulting in incomplete fermentation and wines with higher-than-desired residual sugar levels.

Infections and Microbiological Issues

Inappropriate temperatures can promote the growth of undesirable microorganisms, such as bacteria or wild yeasts, which can negatively affect wine quality and cause undesirable effects.

To avoid all the aforementioned problems, those in charge of the fermentation process typically control and adjust the temperature at which this process takes place, depending on the type of wine they aim to produce, using techniques to cool or heat the grape juice or fermentation tank, if necessary.

Loss of freshness and balance

Another effect of high temperatures is that they can lead to the degradation of natural acids present in the grapes, resulting in wines with lower acidity and freshness.

Astringency and bitterness

High temperatures can extract more astringent tannins from the skins and seeds of the grapes, resulting in wines with an unbalanced structure and an excessively astringent or bitter character.

Pressing

After the fermentation period, the skins, seeds, and solid residues are separated from the liquid. This is achieved using presses that exert pressure on the residues, done with finely adjusted grape presses; instruments that combine precision and delicacy to extract the last drop of essence and any remaining liquid left by the grape seeds and skins. Through gradual pressure, they also separate the solid parts. This step is an art and can make a significant difference in the texture and character of the final wine.

Secondary fermentation

Some wines, such as sparkling wines, undergo a second fermentation to develop natural bubbles. During this secondary fermentation, the wine is sealed in bottles with

yeast and additional sugars, producing the gas that forms the bubbles.

Aging

Photo: Personal library

In this stage, after fermentation, various containers made of different materials are used. Once the juice is transferred to these containers, it is allowed to rest to develop its flavors and characteristics over a period of time that varies depending on the type of wine.

The choice of containers can affect the flavor profile, texture, and complexity of the wine.

Oak barrels

Oak barrels are perhaps the most iconic aging vessels in the wine industry, used for high-quality red and white wines. Oak imparts aromas, flavors, and texture to the wine. During the aging process, specialists can choose between French, American, or other oak varieties that may influence the wine's profile.

Stainless steel tanks

Stainless steel tanks are popular for aging white wines and some red wines. These tanks are ideal for maintaining the freshness and fruity characters of wines, as they do not impart flavors or aromas from the container material. Additionally, they are easy to clean and require minimal maintenance.

Clay or ceramic amphorae

In recent years, the use of clay or ceramic amphorae for wine aging has resurfaced. These containers allow for controlled micro-oxygenation and can add minerals and earthy nuances to the wine.

Concrete tanks

Concrete tanks are used for aging both red and white wines. Porous concrete allows for micro-oxygenation, which can soften tannins and improve the wine's texture. It can also add certain mineral nuances.

Barrels of other wood types

In addition to oak, some wineries in New Mexico may experiment with other wood types for barrels, such as pine. Each type of wood contributes unique aromatic and flavor profiles to the wine.

The choice of aging vessel depends on the winery's philosophy, the type of wine being produced, and the specific characteristics of the grape.

Photo: Río Grande Winery

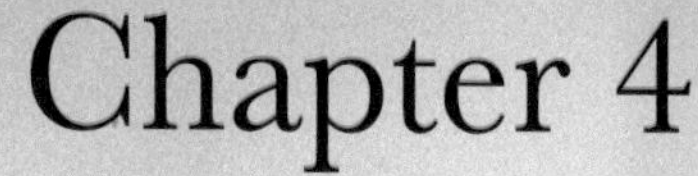

Chapter 4

Wine Making

"Take counsel in wine but resolve afterwards in water."

Benjamin Franklin

Wine Making

Wine blending

Wine blending is both an artistic and technical process in which specialists combine different individual wines to create a final wine that reflects a specific flavor profile and characteristics.

The blending process can take place either before or after aging in barrels and can be applied to red, white, and rosé wines.

Component selection

The specialists evaluate the different individual wines available in the winery, which may come from different vineyards, grape varieties, and different harvests and types of barrels. Each component contributes different flavor profiles, structure, and texture.

Before beginning the blend, a clear objective must be established; it could be creating a balanced wine, improving certain flavor aspects, or expressing a specific style.

Blending Trials

Blending trials are conducted in small quantities to explore how the components interact with each other. This stage is essential for adjusting the proportions of each wine and achieving the desired flavor profile. Multiple combinations and adjustments may be made before finding the ideal blend.

Tasting and Analysis

The blends are tasted, and their characteristics are analyzed: evaluating aroma, taste, acidity, balance, and texture. Additionally, sensory tests and chemical analyses can be performed to ensure quality and consistency.

Final Adjustments

Based on the tasting and analysis results, specialists may make final adjustments to the blend. This may involve changes in component proportions or even the addition of small amounts of other wines to achieve the desired complexity.

Stability and Compatibility

At this stage, it is important to consider how the blend will behave during aging.

Some wines may interact differently with oxygen and other components. Over time, a stable blend that develops attractive flavors and aromas throughout aging is sought.

Final Approval

Once the desired blend is achieved, it is approved, and it is determined whether the blend will age in the same container or be divided into different barrels for aging. Then, when the wine has reached the appropriate maturity, it proceeds to bottling and labeling.

Photo: Mario Murguía y Carlos Rodríguez

Photo: Personal library

Chapter 5

Bottling and Storage

"Good wine is a good familiar creature if it be well used."

William Shakespeare

Bottling and Storage

This step follows a careful process to ensure the quality and authenticity of each bottle.

Wine Preparation

Before bottling, the wine is removed from the barrels or aging tanks, and undergoes chemical and sensory analysis to ensure that it is at its optimal point and meets the quality standards of the winery.

Filtration and Clarification

The wine may undergo filtration and clarification processes to remove any solid particles, which is especially important for wines that will have a long storage period in the bottle.

Bottle Filling

The bottles, previously cleaned and sterilized, are placed on the bottling line, using precise machines controlled manually or mechanically. Each bottle is filled with the exact amount of wine, avoiding oxidation and the formation of air bubbles to preserve the quality of the wine.

Closure and Sealing

Depending on the type of wine and the style of the winery, different types of closures are used, with natural cork stoppers being the most popular for high-end wines, while screw caps may be preferred for younger and fresher wines.

The closure must be airtight to protect the wine from oxygen and ensure its longevity.

Labeling and Capsuling

Filled bottles go through the labeling and capsuling process. Labels are applied with precision and may contain detailed information about the wine: the vintage, variety, and region. Additionally, a capsule (the metallic top covering the bottle neck) is applied to ensure the integrity of the closure and add an aesthetic touch.

Quality Control

Sealed and labeled bottles undergo rigorous quality control processes. Visual inspections are carried out to detect any issues with labels or closures. Random samples are taken for chemical and sensory analysis to ensure that the wine meets established standards.

Storage and Distribution

When it comes to storing freshly bottled grape wine, it is important to meet several conditions to ensure that the wine maintains its freshness and quality during the initial resting period.

Generally, young wine bottles should be stored upright during the first few weeks or months; this allows the wine to come into full contact with the cork and dissipate any residual gas.

Movement or disturbance of newly bottled bottles should be avoided during the first few weeks, as the wine needs time to settle.

It is important to avoid sudden temperature changes; a constant temperature is needed. Bottles are preferably stored in a dark place or in opaque boxes to protect the wine from direct light, which can break down or affect the taste and aroma. To avoid the previous points, storage is done under controlled conditions.

Then, the bottles are sent to retail distributors and restaurants, or they are displayed and tasted at the winery where the entire afore mentioned process took place, where the quality and excellence of each bottle will also be appreciated.

The bottling and labeling process is a combination of advanced technology, manual precision, and a deep commitment to quality at all stages. Each bottle is the result of the passion and dedication of an entire team of experts.

Foto: Dr. Melquiadez

Chapter 6

Pairing and Matching

"Old wood best to burn, old wine to drink, old friends to trust".

Francis Bacon

Pairing and Matching

This concept of "pairing" is also known as "harmony and union": it is the art of combining dishes and wines with a dual purpose; enhancing the characteristics of the different courses of a meal with the reds, whites, and sparkling wines that accompany it, and enjoying a gastronomic experience by uniting similar flavors, sensations, and aromas, always making the most of it. It is important to consider the recommendations of experts in the field, while not forgetting your own taste and desire to experiment with new combinations. Here are some tips that can help you, as they are considered classics.

Red Wine and Red Meat

The art of pairing wine and food is a sensory dance that opens the doors to unforgettable experiences. In each glass and in every bite, we find the magic of flavor harmony.

Photo: Personal library

The proper choice of a wine can elevates a dish in a sublime way, while the food can reveal hidden nuances in a wine. The undeniable relationship and complicity they share create a unique experience with each combination.

Red wines, such as Cabernet Sauvignon, Tempranillo or Malbec, usually pair well with red meats.

Photo: Personal library

White Wine and Fish

Fresh white wines like Chardonnay, Sauvignon Blanc, Gewürztraminer, and Albariño are the perfect complement to fish and seafood dishes as they balance the flavors with their lightness and freshness.

Photo: Personal library

Sweet Wine and Desserts

Excellent companionship for wines made with Muscat, Riesling, Late Harvest, Moscato, and Viognier grapes, together whit desert they make for a spectacular finale.

Sparkling Wine and Appetizers

Sparkling wines are the perfect choice for holidays, with favorites like Champagne and Rosé being excellent accompaniments to appetizers such as nuts, serrano ham, and cheeses.

Each region in the world has its own wine and food pairings, and it's important to consider your preferences. Enjoy savoring the contrasts; observe the colors, aromas, and body of each wine; lift your glass with joy and gratitude for the present moment.

Photo: Personal library

Water

Pairing wine with water is a common practice, and below are the key points to consider:

- It allows your taste buds to cleanse and better appreciate the nuances of each wine.
- It neutralizes residual flavors on the palate.
- It dilules the alcohol in the body, helping to maintain balance and prevent dehydration.

Photo: Jerron Davis, Ruidoso NM

Chapter 7

Experience The Wine Route in New Mexico

Experience The Wine Route in New Mexico

I invite you to embark on a unique wine tourism experience in one of the most exciting wine regions in the United States. Whether you have extensive experience with wines or you're an occasional lover of this magnificent and elegant beverage, or even if you're a curious traveler in search of new adventures, the wineries of New Mexico have something for everyone.

Come and share special moments with friends and family while you indulge in the magic offered by local wines. Explore from the sunny south of the Mesilla Valley to the majestic mountains of the Enchanted Circle in the northern part of the state.

New Mexico hosts an incredible variety of wineries and vineyards ready to offer you a great diversity of landscapes, colors, and incredible flavors. Don't miss the opportunity to discover them; I assure you the surprise will be enormous, and you'll want to come back to share it with those you love the most.

Imagine tasting exceptional wines while immersing yourself in the rich culture, gastronomy, and natural beauty of New Mexico. Each wine region has its own story to tell and its own oenological character to discover. Wineries and vineyards invite you to immerse yourself and awaken your passion for wine with expert-led tastings, tours among the vines, and special events throughout the year.

Are you ready to embark on an unforgettable journey throughout New Mexico?

Next, I'll give you a brief tour of the three regions of the state with the highest wine production:

Mesilla Valley

The Mesilla Valley is located in southern New Mexico, stretching along the Rio Grande and flanked by the majestic Organ Mountains. It is well-known for its sunny and dry climate, perfect for cultivating certain grape varieties that contribute to the production of high-quality wines.

Considered a region with rich cultural and historical heritage, it is a popular destination for those wishing to explore history, gastronomy, and the wine industry. Here, you will enjoy southern hospitality and taste different wines under the warm sun.

During your tour, you'll encounter numerous wines tasting rooms offering excellent service, cleanliness, attention, and breathtaking landscapes comprising valleys, mountains, and incredible sunsets.

You'll be able to enjoy wine in your preferred way, whether alone or accompanied by your favorite people, while listening to live music performed by local artists sharing their talent. It's an experience you shouldn't miss out on.

Photo: Las Cruces NM / By: Aaron Walterscheid

Middle Rio Grande Valley

Located in the heart of New Mexico, both cities, are rich in history and architecture that will undoubtedly captivate you upon visiting, or if you've been here before, you'll want to return to experience it again.

Come explore the fusion of cultural influences that have settled here while sampling wines crafted by expert winemakers who delight in sharing what has sprung from this beautiful land. With landscapes adorned by majestic mountains and fertile farmlands, it's an ideal place to spend time, either alone or with company.

Photo: Santa Fe NM / By: Jerron Davis

 Northern New Mexico

The northern region of New Mexico, nestled along the Rio Grande near Taos, is renowned for its natural beauty, a sparkling starry sky, ancient architecture, and a burgeoning wine scene that's accessible to all. Visit this magical place and savor the variety of wines crafted from locally grown grapes: The experiences in this area are truly unforgettable.

Photo: Tularosa NM / By: Jerron Davis

In this brief tour of the three most emblematic wine-producing regions of New Mexico, ranging from the entrepreneurial spirit of the first vines planted in Mesilla to the growing wine scene in the center, and the artistic charm of the north, my hope is to have sparked your curiosity to explore these areas. Wander and taste the exquisite wines, so similar yet so different from each other, each with the touch of its creator, the region, the land, the care, but above all, the traditions.

🍷 Wine Festivals

Each winery celebrates individually on different dates throughout the year, whether to promote the production of a new wine, the expansion of the winery, new services, promotion of an exclusive club, or the grand celebration of the harvest, where the land is honored for its annual fruits.

The significance of each local celebration highlights the area and becomes a space for discovering, sharing flavors, and aromas.

In addition to these local celebrations, there are Annual Statewide Wine Festivals, where New Mexico wineries have the opportunity to showcase their wine selections to a large number of people. Special prices are promoted, local artisans, food trucks, and live music ensure your entertainment from the moment you arrive. The festivals are held at various locations throughout the state, with the most popular venues being:

- Ruidoso.
- Santa Fe.
- Albuquerque.
- Las Cruces.
- Taos.

Photo by: Aaron Walterscheid

Foto: Aaron Walterscheid

Tasting Rooms

Each wine cellar offers the option to explore its exclusive tasting room, inviting you to live a unique experience that you can sense from the moment you walk through the door.

The ambiance is a perfect blend of elegance and warmth, where you'll find one or more of the owners welcoming you with a friendly smile.

Here, history and passion for wine intertwine spectacularly. In some wine cellars, you can observe oak barrels, exuding that unmistakable aroma of aged wine.

Soft and warm lights highlight the labels of award-winning wines adorning the shelves, each telling its own story. You can hear the sound of glasses tinkling lightly as the experts gracefully pour the liquid into them, creating a musical and welcoming atmosphere.

Your palate is transported on a sensory journey with each sip, a blend of flavors delicately unfolding in your mouth, from the fruity freshness of a white wine to the seductive complexity of a red one.

The vast knowledge of the tasting guides envelops you, offering you a deeper connection with the culture and craftsmanship behind each bottle. All of this combines to provide you with an unforgettable experience, one that captivates your senses and leaves you craving more of this fascinating wine culture.

Chris Baker: Singer, composer, and musician.

Live Music

Upon arriving at a winery in New Mexico, you'll feel the warmth of a unique welcome that invites you to stay and explore, taste, and enjoy its wide variety of wines through flavor, aroma, and color tastings. Additionally, indulge in delicious accompaniments such as charcuterie, appetizers, and regional cuisine. Get ready to enjoy magnificent live music, which enhances the experience, whether you're listening to a band, a cellist, a saxophonist, a guitarist, or a solo musician singing blues, rock, or country music.

Each aspect of these places will provide you with an emotionally rich experience, thanks to the harmony of nature, the activities, and the kindness of the people.

You'll fall in love with the radiant golden sun and its magical ocher-colored sunsets, and the majestic mountains contrasting with lights and shadows. In these places, time seems imperceptible, the routine of daily life is left behind, and problems disappear as if by magic.

Closing

Photo: Personal library

Well, it's 10:00 pm, and here I am again, leaving this wine cellar where I've had some great moments. As I close the door behind me, the conversations, jokes, and empty glasses remain.

Today, I had the pleasure of enjoying incredible live music while indulging in a delicious piece of tiramisu — a delightful dessert, smooth as silk — with a subtle hint of coffee liqueur, it's my favorite, paired with a glass of wine. These two flavors intertwine in my mouth, creating an enveloping and seductive explosion; they seem like the perfect combination to me.

As I walk, I observe the starry sky; there's not a day that I'm not impressed by the beautiful landscapes that nature offers us. Sometimes I feel like my eyes are insufficient to capture the full extent of its majesty. How wonderful it is to be alive!

In the distance, I hear the murmurs of people leaving shortly after me. Most of them talk and laugh, but there are also some, like me, who walk in silence. However, they don't seem to look around; perhaps their minds didn't manage to clear up, but there will be another occasion to try again.

The sounds emitted by some nocturnal animals are interesting and curious. I try to identify where they come from, but they seem to be everywhere, even if I can't see them. As I continue walking, I contemplate the rows of vineyards, perfectly aligned and bathed in the silver light of the moon. I can't help but think that they will gift us their delicious juice in the next harvest.

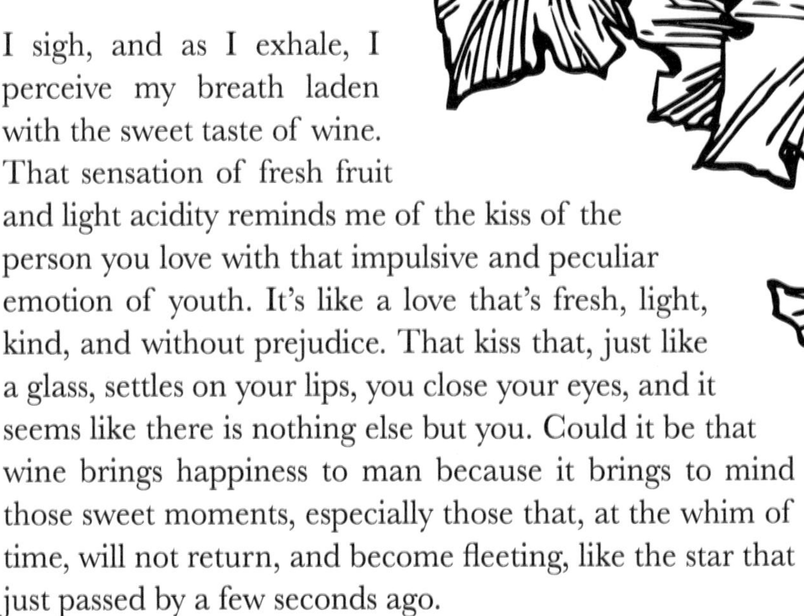

I sigh, and as I exhale, I perceive my breath laden with the sweet taste of wine. That sensation of fresh fruit and light acidity reminds me of the kiss of the person you love with that impulsive and peculiar emotion of youth. It's like a love that's fresh, light, kind, and without prejudice. That kiss that, just like a glass, settles on your lips, you close your eyes, and it seems like there is nothing else but you. Could it be that wine brings happiness to man because it brings to mind those sweet moments, especially those that, at the whim of time, will not return, and become fleeting, like the star that just passed by a few seconds ago.

How wonderful life is! How tranquil it feels! One thing I'm sure of: this is one of the moments that I'll carry engraved in my memory until infinity claims me, with it I'll give color to my gray moments.

The howling of a coyote in the distance makes me react… It's time to return to reality. I get into my car and drive back home, smiling at everything, and at nothing.

Sources:

https://viticulture.nmsu.edu

https://viticulture.nmsu.edu/history.html

https://nmwine.com

https://www.mesillanm.gov/history

https://www.nnmvinewine.org

https://pubs.nmsu.edu/_circulars/CR483/index.html

Made in the USA
Columbia, SC
06 July 2024

38137493R00053